VOICES

BREAKING THE CHAINS OF PAIN THROUGH POETRY

———————

SHANIA KERINA

Voices: Breaking the Chains of Pain Through Poetry
©2026

By
Shania Kerina

alurepublishingllc@gmail.com
www.alurepublishing.net

ISBN: 979-8-9987951-5-2 (Paperback)
Publication Date: March 28, 2026

Dedication

For my sons, Kimani and Nolan.
For my parents.
Most importantly, for myself.

I never thought I had the courage to share myself this deeply. Doing events and speaking, that's
one thing but expressing myself in this magnitude is scary. I have been growing, glowing, and
becoming for a long time. Truth is, becoming is a constant journey. If you would have told 23
year old Shania who was pregnant, homeless, and hopeless, that she would be here, I do not
think I would have believed you. And what is here? Healing, loving life, joyful, mothering, and
BECOMING my best self.
This book, these are OUR Voices. Each poem represents someone, somewhere out in the
world who may have felt or been where I have been. Raw. Real.
This book is not structured because, well, our thoughts are not.
Each poem is powerful, it is love, it is God's grace, it is all the beautiful things that make me who
I am and I am so excited to share it with you. Thank you for going on this journey with me.
Proverbs 3:5-6, "Trust in the Lord with all your heart and lean not on your own
understanding; in all your ways submit to him, and he will make your paths straight"

Contents

Who Am I

Where did I come from?
I came from deception
Lies that run deep
Generation to Generation
Where the lies once was my truth
I came from jealousy
Family who wants to see you do good but just not better
than them but if you do do better .
Watch your back
Because I also came from slander and your name will
be drug through the mud if you even think
about setting a boundary
I came from failed promises and butt whoopings
because the strength of the household on one
is too much and they need a release so you're the
punching bag
I came from grief
But we don't talk about that
I came from a place where we don't talk about the
losses or the heartbreak or the heartaches
When your heart is aching and you just close off
You hide behind the closed doors
Cry in your pillow
Wipe your eyes and walk out that room as if you're okay
I came from brokenness
Poor spending habits
I came from spend your last dollar to erase the last
memory away
I came alcohol addiction ,coping addiction
Addicted to running away from the pain vs confronting it

I came from Undiagnosed mental illnesses
I came from not knowing

I came from being too light skinned to fit in with friends
Too light skinned to be African
So wondering where do I fit in
God Where do I come from
Because what if I came from a place of peace or joy but
it's just been sucked out of me because
when the lights were dim around me they needed an
energy source
God told me Those are the places I came from
But now I come from freedom
I come from Joy in the morning and peaceful rest
I come from healthy boundaries and communication
I come from knowing who my daddy is
So Thank you God for making sure I didn't become my
environment
Equipped with the full armor of God,
Thank you for the belt of truth buckled around my waist
The thoughts that run deep into my mind
"You are not enough"
"You won't succeed"
Those are lies but God you are my truth
& Depression you no longer have a home here
I had to put on the breastplate of righteousness ,
because my heart was hardening but God I
thank you for softening it
You made me better instead of bitter
Making my pain a passage
My feet now fitted with readiness that comes from the
gospel of peace
I took up the shield of faith,

Trusting God to make a way out of no way
Robbing Peter to pay Paul some days

While I am building a business on blind faith
God are you sure that this mess is supposed to be my
message ?
Helmet of salvation and the sword of the Spirit, God
your word keeps me lifted.
And I've been learning to pray in the Spirit
I'm grateful I didn't have to be perfect
I didn't need to know all the answers
It was no more why me but instead why not me
So God Thank you for putting the pieces back together
You knew who I was before the womb and all i had to
do was Trust and believe in you
You see This was a talk about the journey
The journey of more
The journey of chasing dreams and shifting seems
Shifting perspective
When God calls you to do a thing
No one can name you or that thing but Him
Homelessness wasn't my name
The suicide attempts
The rape
The rejection
I now come from forgiveness and lifting as I climb and
I'm grateful
so I want you to hear me and know , God changed my
name , and he can change yours too

Survivor

This is a trigger warning
I attempted suicide when I was a junior in college and
some one asked me how did I know I
wanted to end it all
I told her I was tired
Listen my world looked black
I no longer had the energy to live
My smile became fake
And I was drowning in my tears
You see The store of spirits became my best friend
I was drinking almost a bottle a day
And at 20 I wanted out
I was hurting
God you keep taking people from my life
Trauma keeps showing up at my front door
I'm tired of the abusive relationships
I am tired of being punched down
And
I remember my friend knocking on that same door of
those traumas
I watched the tears flow from her eyes
And she said
"Shania , YOU ARE HURTING US.
What is wrong with you ?
I couldn't gather my words and I cried and cried and
cried
I cried because for the first time
Someone saw me
They saw my pain
She saw I wasn't my normal energy

She saw how my appearance declined
And my smile disappeared
Y'all see a beautiful women but y'all don't see my pain
Y'all see a smile and how I own a room but you aren't in
the room at night when I can barely
calm the anxiety attacks or the tears
Y'all aren't in the room where the tissue is by my
bedside and I can hardly get up
If this poem resonates with you
This poem is for you
I had to learn that all the trauma
All the abuse
All the past adversities I had to endure are the very
things that helped me to BECOME who I am
today
Then some ask me how do you keep going

Psalms 147-3 "there it go" he heals the brokenhearted
and binds up their wounds and while I
reveal my scars to you I allow God to nurse my wounds
that are still present
So to the mom who is overstimulated and feels like
giving up
To the man who feels the world is on his shoulders and
it's hard for him to breathe
To the women and the men that have been , the
molestation , the abuse
To those struggling with hyper sexuality because of that
abuse
Please know It is not your identity
To the one who is burnt out from trying to build that
business
To the person overworked trying to make ends meet

To whoever feels alone
You are going through life
You feel like there is no sunshine to your cloudy day
I just want you to know that I see you
You are loved
You have purpose here and your story is not over yet
I'm in therapy
I work out now
I eat better
I have different coaches but I had to become aware of
what was drowning me so I could survive
So I could take back my power
Now it's your turn to save you
You are capable
You are worthy
And everything you feel you need you already have
within you
I know the cliche saying of you got this but you do
Conquer it and don't let it conquer you

Superhero

Vulnerability and self awareness are my super powers
I am able to say I'm not ok
While giving grace to myself and the emotions that
come
To some, that is a weakness
Speaking of emotions , crying , taking a break , is a
"sign" makes you inferior to them
You see I decided to stop letting depression to control
my mind like Loki
Instead I became iron man and found a way to heal my
bruised heart
I became Diana and had no wonder for peoples
thoughts on journey of becoming whole
Did you know Black Panther could sense fear and lies ?
I had to learn discernment
I had to allow God to become Captain of my story as he
shielded me from the attacks
I had to have a Hawkeye
I needed to be able to see the vision God had for my life
and understand that my mess would
soon become my message
You know visions can be tormented so be careful of the
ultrons, excuse me villains, that you
have around you
Be weary of your circle
You want people around you who know you are
purposes
Who will avenge you
Who will be an iron fist for you when you're too weak to
fight the fight yourself

I'm grateful God needed me to become my own savior
Because I have learned how to save myself so I can
save others
You see I am not afraid to face sadness
I am not afraid to go through the dark and go neck and
neck with my fears
I once allowed depression to almost win but I now I
have the upper hand
Why ? Because I'm a superhero
Just know all survivors don't wear a cape

Breaking Point

Imagine finally cracking
You can't think
And Sometimes you can't breathe and you are in a
constant battle with your mind
Things are unclear
Do I pray away the mental illness or do I take the
medication
Do I suppress the depression or seek the necessary
help I need despite my church telling me
it's just spirits
Ohhhhh I'm confused
And it sucks because technically I'm already confused
and this doesn't make it any easier
Confused on why I had to
Go through so much trauma to the point I'm imbalanced
Suicide ain't an option like it was at 20 I have kids now
Confused on why God continues to think I'm his
strongest soldier
Confused on why I gotta fight you and you and I'm just
trying to be a better mother
Even better than the mother I lost and never got to
Experience
And well that's confusing because what am I comparing
my motherhood journey to when I
didn't get to have one
Man sometimes I don't even know if I want to just lay
I need to put the bottle down
Do I take a shower
Do I wash the dishes that have piled up
Before putting away all the dishes that have been

washed for days
Do I pick up the laundry that have flooded my office
Because I'm at a point where I'm tired and a nap can't
fix that
A nap can't help the racing thoughts
Or The crying spells
I'm barely eating
I Can't sleep
I cracked
But you crack
We all crack
We all need rest
We all need community
We all need hope
But I hope you remember that with cracking comes
rebirth
You are born again and made anew
Listen i Have a therapist but I decided to Trust him so
he can quiet my mind
He heals the brokenhearted and binds up their wounds
so know that
God would never put you through what he hasn't
prepared you for

Let Him Work

I feel sometimes we can underestimate God
There is nothing to hard Too far too wide
There is nothing he can not do
I question him often
I get in his way,
I've interfered far too many times with his plan over my
life
I felt he was moving too slow
I didn't like what I seeing
I wanted more and I wanted it now
This morning I had a moment
I was in my feelings and was questioning God on some
things and he said remember what I
brought you through ?
Don't think I'll ever leave or forsake you
So I had to rewind the tape
Times I've almost died
Grief
Loss
Rejection
Hopelessness
Every time I was Terrified you kept me
Or what about the suicide attempts
What about the abusive relationships
What about all the deaths and losses
My list could go on
And I think we forget and need a reminder so I'll say it
again
There is NOTHING and I mean nothing too hard for my
God

The way he brought you through it before he'll do it
again so just how you give that nigga in your
phone 1,000 chances knowing he's no good or just like
you know that woman only wants to use
you or whatever y'all got going on but you take her back
Give God those SAME chances but more
Rest in him
Let him lead you,
Allow him to show you what you deserve , let him show
you your portion
Because You deserve that

Boy who cried wolf

To some I'm like the boy who cried wolf
You know that story
The boy who would continuously cry wolf
It wasn't true
But then when the wolf came it was too late
I cried boundaries
I cried peace but I still allowed people to stay too long
I cried empty promises to myself
Promising this vessel of mine that I was divine
and worthy of love and peace but never following
through
So when I finally followed through with my boundaries it
was too late
I am now the villain in many stories because I am firm to
my boundaries
I speak a different language
My "relationships" couldn't hold the wait of what I
needed but I realized it wasn't my job to get
people to understand them
My job was to stand in them
Stand firm
Be true to me
So to some I was the boy who cried wolf
And that's okay
Because in my story I defeated the wolf
The thing that scared me
You see when you set boundaries you have to be ready
to be alone
And I don't like that
You have to be ready for people to want to go against

them but you deserve peace
So in my story
I cried wolf but I conquered him too

Freedom Love

They say when a woman is loved correctly
She becomes 10x the women she's meant to be
She becomes greater
She is ready to take on the world
Knowing that she has a soft place to land
Experiencing a love so sweet
Those past traumas know they have no place in her
land
The baggage she carried emptied themselves
& she had the space she needed to live
As she deserves
When a woman is loved correctly,
she loves you back in a way you could have never
imagined
The safe space she holds for you
The passionate love making that awaits for you
When you make your woman feel loved
Beautiful
Cared for and Heard
Know the RIGHT woman will reciprocate that and more

Black Hurt

Dear black man
One day I'll be a wife
Your wife
I'll be folding your laundry
Cook your food
Make our bed
Bear our kids while raising them alongside with you
Future leaders entrepreneurs doctors lawyers whatever
their hearts desire
I want to do so much with you but yet
you're so busy looking for Ms Parker
And I want to know do you honestly see the hurt that
has been parked right here right on my
heart
For some reason I am the most disrespected by you
We are the most disrespected
Black women
Our queens
Mothers
Amongst our own people at that , amongst you
As black women we stand on the forefront for you
But we are tormented, belittled, abused
Not by all
But by those who have not either dealt with their pain or
Are still going through the rollercoaster of life
Because we are bold in who we are, it frightens so
many
But I am not your punching bag we are not your
punching bag
I am not the person you take your anger out on because

you don't know where to
Direct it
I am not the person you get to belittle because
someone made you feel small
I am not your mother so don't think because you have
unhealed mommy wounds I will pick up
the pieces she left behind
I am not here to stroke you or your ego because I am
not your cum bucket while all you come
with is heartbreak and pain
I am so much more than a cute face in vein
So, Dear Black Man
Can you remind me what it feels like to be safe
remind me that not all men rape
Remind me that you all do not abuse their queens
That they uplift and inspire
Or nurture and
Dear black man remind what I feels like to be whole
again
I was once daddy's little girl , a princess

Now I've drifted off into the Black Sea where all I see
and feel Is pain and suffering
Negro show me the mutha loving game if it's just going
to continue to be a never ending cycle of
love hurt or find a new prey
But King show me what it feels like to be a Queen
behind you as my strong black man
As my knight
as the head of our household
Show me strength
I will bring the peace but stop leaving me in pieces

Ultimate

I lost my power when I thought man could love me more
than God, more than myself, thinking
that things of the world would make me feel immortal ,
wanting the trauma sucked from my body
So immensely that I I allowed too many people in my
space
Trying to drown out the pain
You see i lost my power
My strength
God I know you didn't bring me this far to only bring me
this far
You wouldn't leave me here
What is going on because I am suffering
& I find myself curled up under blankets more than I find
myself in my prayer room
Did God abandon me like my parents did ?
Or drop me like my family ?
God did you allow him to take my innocence and ruin
my femininity ?
God why did you allow me to go through so much pain
and suffering
Then I get a call
I hear this soft voice through the phone and she asks
"Hey girl ! where you been "
Then all she heard was my tears
She said Shania understand When you are called God
will always come get you so get up
And I want you to hear me , "Get up"
For those listening to my words GET UP
The devil can't have you

He can't have your mind
He can't have your family
He can't have your gifts
Get up because I want you to
See yourself how god sees YOU
Not how you think your trauma has defined you
Or the world defines you
See you were created you in his image
So what does that mean ?
You are FEARLESS
You are impeccable
You are love and you are loved
There is a light that shines bright within you
And you have every right to the blessings God has upon
your life
So Get up
Stand in your strength
Stand in your faith
And know you are not alone in this battle

Love Letter

This is my love letter to you
& I just want to love you
I want to Be your peace after a hard day
Kiss on your scars
Baby God will nurse your wounds but I want to be able
to put the bandages on for you after
I want to affirm you on a day to day basis
I want to Pray over you
Pour into you so you are only giving from your saucer
and not an empty cup
I want to Adjust your crown when you feel defeated
Wash it
Polish it
Place it back on to your mantle
I want be the big spoon for you if you need me to
And though I'm 5'2
My heart weighs 252
And know that any of this doesn't take away from who
you are or your strength
How I see you
How I will submit to you
Honor you
Respect you
Me being able to serve you just reminds me of the Safe
space you've created for me to land
How you have never judged me and loved me
How you've honored my mental and respected my
mantle
How you never called me sensitive but loved on my
emotions with me

Allowed me to the the boss and a baby at the same
time
I want to pour into you just how you do me
The days you cry in the car behind that steering wheel ,
i see you
The shower cries , i see you
And I want to pass you the tissue
And if you need a moment , I want to be waiting for you
Place your head on my chest and be what you need me
to be in that moment
Thank you for pressing forward
Thank you for carrying the weight
Thank you for always being my strength but understand
I'm yours too
I love you
Yesterday
Today
Tomorrow
And forever

Childhood Trauma

I saw this post the other day that said "severe early
childhood trauma creates a child with
intense coping mechanisms"
I was 14 when I started working
Taking care of what I needed to
I know now that grandma was only doing what she
could with what she was given
I was 15 when I experienced one of multiple traumatic
events which caused me to hate men
I was 16 when I had three boyfriends
One for my phone
One for food
And one for clothes
The streets started raising me
You know , teaching me skills I would need eventually
So when at 23 I was kicked out , pregnant and
homeless, I figured it out
GOD helped me figure it out
I skipped some story times
But when you say to me
"Wow Shania , you are so mature for your age" I need
you to hear me loud and clear
If my strength could speak
She would want you to know it's
That's the survival you hear in my voice
It's the 12 year old girl who felt rejected and was
bruised
It's the 20 year old girl who tried to end it all
It's the 23 year old girl pregnant and homeless
It's the 25 year old girl who found out she was pregnant

after leaving and moving to a new state
It's survival you hear
It's pain
You hear all the nights I cried and had to nurse myself
back to health
You hear me learning to ground myself during anxiety
attacks
You hear me bleeding but I'm so good with my words
that I just sound mature and like I have it
all together
Now at 29 God is healing me
I deserve a soft life so I am speaking that over myself
While I move and speak in love
I am speaking in strength and not in fear of rejection but
you know what they say only God can
judge me so who are you ?
Today , to anyone listening to the sound of my voice ,
I'm sorry you had to be strong so young .
I'm sorry you had to wipe your own tears and cheer
yourself on
Crazy thing is , I just am understanding that it was
always God
It was God who gave me that extra strength
It was God who sent resources my way mother and
father figures
My social workers and coaches

my ex boyfriends momma, and even my professors
When you take a second a REAL second to reflect...yes
we may have had to grow up quickly
and felt alone but God placed people on our journey for
us. Think of all the times he saved us .
So we actually were never really alone were we ?

I just want you to know You're okay now
You're okay
And if you haven't heard it or even if you have
Know that I love you
Even if you're struggling to love yourself
Piece

Why me?

I felt God was forcing me to understand my pain : Why
me God?
Why do you feel I am the one who can endure so much
pain
Why am I supposed to be the messenger of this story
where i fell there is no glory
Why did you take my mother, the one who is supposed
to be my rock and my best friend
Or My father, the first man that loved me and will always
love me. Who is supposed to scare all
the guys away and then walk me down the aisle
Or how about taking someone who I loved so sweetly ,
called me beautiful every chance he got
All of them gone too soon
But How could you let a man take my innocence from
me and
then allow him to brag that he "hit" this ?
You know when you say no that actually means no
I guess my tears didn't mean a thing, or saying get off
As long as he busted a nut and added a count he was
okay
How could you allow me to be so broken, so bitter
God You are always supposed to be there and there
are so many times you left me alone
cold, torn and ashamed
There is not on ounce of love I have for myself
how can anyone else love me
this broken soul
I felt you didn't even love me
If you loved me all of this would not have happened to

me
Men that have had my body
but left me with a big hole in my heart.
God what am I searching for
Why me ? Why am I going through all of this
You see me hurting and to the top of my lungs I just
want to scream I hate you so the heavens
can hear
Why do I feel alone in a crowded room
Sometimes I want to pop all the medicine in the cabinet,
get that knife and slice up and down
until I can no longer feel, how about russian roulette, or
maybe jump in front of a moving vehicle.
Yeah that's what I think about, ending this precious life
of mine
But I never stopped to think where am I now?
I am a graduate, why am I alive , I am living proof that I
can do all things through Christ.
God you are the way the truth and the light
My love, my missing piece but I still continue to run from
No man could ever love me the way you do
You have saved me so many countless times that I
should be asking why not me
Why should I not be the vessel to save someone else
Someday I just have to stop being selfish
God's been available, I never called on him just cussed
at him
Why haven't I understood that he is the strength that I'll
forever need

Let's take a mental PAUSE.

So many emotions. So many words. I used to ask God
why he put me through so much but then
I started to understand it was not for me. It was for you.
The person reading this book. God was
building my character. He was pruning me as he was
preparing me for what was next. I used to
feel that all of my life's hardships disqualified me from
the promises God had for me. I felt dirty. I
felt ashamed. I felt like I just wanted to hide. Success
scared me. Why? Because that means a
light would shine and people could see my flaws in real
time. BUT NOW ! I am in love with who I
am in every aspect. All of the emotions. I legit had to
crawl into God's lap and ask him to take
ALL of it. I needed to see myself how he saw me. I
needed to face emotions and pain that were
buried. Bit by bit. Day by day. On my own time.
Here are some journal prompts that you can sit with that
have helped me on my own journey:
What are some ways I have been holding myself back?
What are some scriptures or quotes I can write down?
(This is good to be able to refer back to them when you
feel you are in a funk)
Who are the people around me? Do I need to
reevaluate my circle?
In what ways can I forgive myself so I can love myself
wholeheartedly?
Maybe even try to create your own.
Breathe.

Take a pause.
You are doing great.

Friendship Rant

Stop trying to be my friend because of trauma
The words I speak are things I've healed from and
healing from and I am not choosing to stay in
that space
So stop trying to be my friend because you want my
energy
Because on my bad days when the energy is dwindling
where are you to spark the flame
Stop trying to be my friend because I'm a giver
I will give you the clothes off of my back
Feed you
Fund you
Drive you
House you
I will give you as much love as I possibly can
But when I'm in need , I'm met with grunts or
aggravation
Side eyes and smirks
Now I do understand that not every friend is a friend but
Stop trying to be my friend because you think I'm strong
and I won't need you to show up for me
To be there for me
Listen I worked hard on this light
I made sure the trauma didn't harden my heart so I can
still receive and give love
I made sure to uproot the necessary baggage so I do
not interpret things from an aching wound
Yes I am strong enough to bear the children
I am strong enough to build the business
I am strong enough to wear the titles and the hats while

still bleeding and allowing God to put
me back together
But just because I'm STRONG that doesn't mean I am
not human
Doesn't mean i am not Fragile
That doesn't mean I don't bruise or break
That doesn't mean I don't cry or get depressed
So stop trying to suck away that strength selfishly
The strength I've built of embracing the emotions while
allowing God to bandage them
The strength of being able to be a light while I guide
myself out of darkness
Stop using me
Because when the time comes for accountability all you
will do is take into account nothing
But we probably can't be friends anyway !
I'm going to make you want to be your best self
To heal
To love
And that scares you
It makes you uncomfortable
Don't get this sweet voiced messed up
I want to comfort you when you mess up and push you
to get up so you can glow up

I don't need friends that envy how people love and
support me or simply just because I fall but
never stay down
I don't want moochers
I don't want friends that abuse grace
I don't want friends that take from me without pouring in
So if this means allowing myself to be
The Villain in your story for finally setting the necessary

boundaries and putting my foot down
then so be it
but I know I'm the hero in another story:
My own

Dependent

I still have flashbacks
the weight on my back from that man and the tears that
soaked the sheets
That night is when I met my first dependent
Burnette, Burnette welcomed me with open arms that
night
From burnie , I don't think I ever been so clear in mixing
the everclear with my favorite chaser
just to chase the repeated memories out of my mind
But trust and believe the pain and the trauma , she
always spinned the block and found comfort
in a new location each time she came back
Then came Pat
Patron always used to take me to visit uncle earl but
because he didn't cause me any trouble
the next morning , he became my comfort And we
kicked it for some years
But you know trauma sometimes doesn't allow you to
keep still so I had to move on to my next
dependent
And then I tried Mary, her and I didn't really fit
she thought she had a way of calming my nerves , she
always had me tripping
So you mean to tell me From Burnette, to Patron , to
Mary, then Paul , then Henry
All these people have all had their way with me
And yet each morning I still woke up to the same
trauma , the same pain
I just kept trying to black out to forget the pain that has
blacked out where my heart should be

I kept running away from the memories that kept
replaying in my head over and and over
I just wanted to cope
And Lately , lately
I've been allowing Captain Morgan to steer my ship
And I am finally releasing my anchor
Letting it fall down and saying ENOUGH is ENOUGH
I am saying that I no longer need to wait for my pain to
spin the block when I can meet her at
the corner and show her that I own the block and there
is no place for her here
But God I just want to know
How Through all of this you still allow me to crawl back
into your lap
They say when a woman experiences a certain trauma
she goes two ways and I went a way
where I spiraled out of control and was controlled by
something just so I could feel good and
forget
but God
thank you for loving me
Thank you for being dependable and available even
when I was depending on everything else
to nurse my wounds back to health
Thank you for being My escape and my safe space to
land when my mind is clouded and I feel
like I can't breathe
God thank you for taking me back
When everyone else just wanted to see my back
whether that was on all 4s or at rock bottom
You picked me back up and showed me my worth
So God Thank you for being the true dependent.

Me Too

It's because of you I say me too
As a father now
I pray your daughter never has to go through what you
put me through
Because you see I blamed myself
That trickled into all my actions and decisions and now
we're here
God did I have to go through this
I know you give your hardest battles to your strongest
soldiers but did you mean this right here
I've been hurting
I been choosing different people to try to fill a void that
you caused
That you burned within my chest
And though I'm a mess
I'm far more capable of pain due to THIS mess
You see I been getting triggered
Angry and some more
The smallest things can set me off but I still hate you
I just want to know when your respect for me when out
the window
I'm not sure if it was when you told your cousin you hit
that when in reality you took that
Or when you slid in my best friends DMs
I will never forget that day
You said "why you so mad it's not like I raped you" I
remember tears falling down my face
because I can still hear the nos I can still feel your
heavy body on top of mine while those tears
leaked onto your bed sheets

I still get chills
I never been the same since
I haven't had the same heart
The same love
Because of you I lost my femininity
Now here I am mom of 2 and searching for my soft side
because I turned to dogging niggas ,
being dogged , instead of allowing love to exist
I don't know when I'll be able to forgive you
But I'll pray for you

Evolving

I could have not pursued my purpose because of all the
hoe mess I used to do
They say a woman goes one of two ways after having it
snatched away
And I went my own way
Afraid of judgement and laughs but y'all knew pained
Shania
Broken Shania
The Shania that wanted to be loved so bad she kept
accepting y'all lil 30 seconds
Used to turn to the bottle so much that I barely even
remember it
but see y'all don't know me nowadays
Just test trials and experiments
My future husband is going to be lucky getting a woman
with all of this experience
I'm not perfect But I'm worth it
And as cliche as it sounds , you know it to too
Just by listening to my words and watching my posture
Seeing the flow of my movement, God has been
molding me for you
So don't excuse me miss
disturbing my hips
As i sway forward towards my resurrection
My rising
My becoming
My healing
My growth
As I raise my beautiful black boys
Don't disturb my peace

Leave me be
I'm tired of the distractions
You don't have much to say to me anyway
You just like my energy
My spirit
But can you feed me the way I have be feeding you
Can you pray for me the way I have done you
Or are you here to just take ?
Let me know

You First

Can I tell you how Today Shania chose herself
She decided She no longer wanted to be in bondage
Chained to bad coping mechanisms
Messed up men
Messed up women
Falling in love so She wouldn't be alone
Staying busy so She don't have to confront that deep
ocean of sadness that causes her
breakdowns
You see Shania chose To release
To love
Not just love herself but to love all the flaws and
insecurities that people have even used against
her
To forgive herself for pain caused by others then
Given to others
Today She chose pumpkin
A nickname given to her by her family
She was The insecure little girl who never forgave
herself
It's not your fault that they had to leave you
It's not your fault that he took your innocence
It's not your fault for all the failed relationships
for all the trauma
Its not your fault
So Just keep going
Keep choosing you
Why ?
Because Your sons deserves the best version of you as
their mother

They deserve A woman who decided to stop neglecting
her feelings and heal
A woman who decided her body was a temple and that
not everybody should have her because
she's scared of lonely
A woman who kilt old habits To set herself free
A woman who understands that she was chosen by
God to carry out something so precious
But you deserve it for yourself sis
Just know I love you
Know you are enough
And just know you the sugar honey and don't let nobody
dim your light

Condolences

Right now I give you my condolences
Because your ego is too big to confront your inner
Demons
To the point where you pinpoint them on me
To make you feel better
To make you feel worthy
So you would rather kill someone else and their image
vs killing the old you to be better
So I pray for you
I pray you find peace in your madness and peace in
your sadness
I pray you find you
I pray for the wicked souls that have ridden in your back
seat because you were to afraid to end
the hack
I pray for the trauma that has consumed you to the point
where you no longer feel you have an
identity
I pray for the mask to come off that you have hidden
behind because you felt weak as a man if
you showed your emotions
I pray you find love
The type of love that will release you from guilt and
shame
The type of love that won't hurt you like you've done me
and we were supposed to be family
The love you were always so egotistical to give
The love you think would fill that black hole where your
heart should be
I pray you reap all the seeds you have sown in the most

genuine way
Why? Because i still think You deserve the world
And despite you trying to tear apart my world and rip the
ground from under my feet I still hope
the best for you
I want you to understand that You are only as strong as
the awareness of your weaknesses
And I guess that's the difference between me and you
I'm healing and you're dealing
But You should just choose .

Mantle

I have been so consumed with finding my man my man
my man
That I forgot about my mantle
And I don't mean the shelf above the fireplace
But my position and my power
There it goes
I've had piece to piece , looking for my peace when it
was always right in front of me
A reflection
My peace was staring right back at me but I was too
blind to see that it was me that could save
me

Forgive me

I'm sorry to those I pushed away because I was loving
you through my trauma
Not understanding that sometimes I was too hard up
and that this hard shell of mine needed to
be broken
But I was broken
In pieces
A tiny million little specs waiting for someone to tell me
"I got you"
"I hear you"
"Let your guard down"
You know all that cute stuff but affirming stuff
Waiting for someone to love me softly and with my love
languages
You see
I used to love to hug and hold hands
When did I get to a point where I felt hugging made me
weak ?
You see when I say broken , I don't mean a little bit
I been pushed down slapped around bruised beaten
and slain
Words and fist to the point I didn't even know I could
love again until I had my kids
Guess God felt I needed extra love
And As I heal and allow God to put the pieces back
together I realized that I couldn't love
through all that unhealed trauma
As a masterpiece I have to master peace and that's still
a process for me
Unlearning to relearn

Refilling after pouring out so much
But to my future person
The man that I pray for every day
Who I journal to
Who I ask God to cover on a day to day to basis
I'm here
Gods molding me for you
So be patient for me
Be patient with me
Know that We don't have much longer in these ghetto
streets

Never Ending

This is for the up and down folks
People who always feel something is up next
I am someone who gets overstimulated
And sometimes I need a moment
I can't answer the phone like I used to or kick it until
4am
I can't be your free therapist and allow you to trauma
dump on me because I feel guilty
When I know what it feels like to be alone
I just can't do a lot of things
My brain is always on a thousand
I'm always thinking of what's next
The kitchen is next
The crumbs under the high chair are next
The clothes piled up in both rooms that need to be
folded are next
Thank y'all for always telling my hat game is on fleek
but that's because I never have the time to
do my own hair next
But now
I'm next
My emotions are next
I am so tired of thinking what is next that there us not a
next to this

No Boundaries

You know what I struggle with
Being too available
I answer the calls
The text
The FaceTimes
People are confused when I don't
Poor boundary setting
I know I know
But I'm working on it
There are certain people in my life where the
boundaries are so thick you couldn't cut with a
knife but there are others where I'm still so sensitive to
them
I don't want to lose them
I hate losing people
Having to grieve people that are still here
That i can still see
It's hard
But it's necessary for my peace of my mind because
right now things are a little foggy
I'm too available and I don't like how you treat me
And when I express this you want to desensitize this as
if I'm tripping
But I ain't

Sister, Sister

Sisterhood has no age
Whether you're 27
43
52
There also is no color for sisterhood
White
yellow
Brown
Orange
Pink
Best thing of all, the blood in our veins does not have to
make you a sister
From Conversations like HEYYYYY GIRLLLLLL
To
Girl Put your big girl panties on and get it done
Or just the plain ole
GirlYou so crazy
Shout out to the Sisters that Wipe your tears when you
feel your back is on the wall
The sisters who are a solid place to land for those of us
that need safety
The sisters who dance with you like there's no one
watching
But To my sisters
All my sisters
I want to say Thank you
Thank you for the random late night calls when the
tears are rolling down my face
Thank you for believing in the dreams and supporting
Rooting always

Thanks to those that show me that motherhood can be beautiful despite the circumstances
For showing me that JOY is a choice and it's my choice !!
Thank you for the laughter that makes my stomach hurt
Thank you for always letting me know wassup and telling me like it is WITH love
Thanks for teaching me accountability without yanking my crown
Sisters represent so many things to so many different people but most of all
To my sister , Thank you for being a light
For Rooting for others
For Loving others, For Showing up for others
For Being present for others no matter WHAT you are going through
Smiles that light up a room
Thank you for a glow that last a lifetime
To GLOW means to give light without flame
So when your down and your flame may be out for a moment,
Remember your light lives on forever through the lives you've impacted
Your sisters got you
Continue to shine your light sis

Lukewarm

If you would have told me years ago I'd finally stop
being lukewarm, I'd probably chuckle
I enjoyed straddling the fence
Know that God loves me unconditionally but I can do
what I do and he's just forgive but nah
That's the wrong mindset to have
Let's look at God as a physical father
He answers the phone every time I Cal
Might not be on the first ring but best believe he won't
leave me nor forsake me
I can call my daddy when I'm in a fight
Demon on my left and one to the right
But my daddy comes in time of war
Because he fights for me
He's the ultimate protector
He is king of kings and lord of lords
Demons tremble I call my daddy's name
Why would I not be faithful to that
Being faithful to the worldly pleasures that's out to steal
kill and destroy
When God is love and wants me to live
But God , thank you for keeping me
All the times I tried to end it
Drinking myself in a pit
Living with no regrets , thank you for saving your
daughter
You knew I was purposed
You knew that one day, today
I'd be talking to your sons and daughters
Encouraging them to heal and equipping them with the

necessary tools needed to take their first
step
When you gave me a child you also blessed me twice
With ideas and vision
You added on to my person and for that I will never step
worshiping you out loud

Alter Ego

So there's this chick named Amber
She real loud
Real bold
Real confident
Can be bossy
Can be messy
Can be funny
Can be emotional, really emotional
Just depends on the dependent of choice she chose
that night
Amber was created when Shania felt she no longer had
a voice
First blackout at 15
She wanted an escape
and nowI'm realizing I no longer need Amber
I no longer need to feel that the alcohol makes me fun
I no longer need an alter ego to alter the perception of
me
I no longer need to feel that that liquor will help me
escape the problems that would still be
present in the morning
I no longer hated Shania
I longer hated her choices
I no longer hated her pain and brokenness
I'm forgiving Shania
I'm creating a safe space for her to know that all the
times she was dropped it wasn't in vain
Gods greatest creations are the broken because light
beams through our cracks
We shine boldly

You can tell when God has brought you through a thing because of how Gentle we can become
You know how God restored what Job lost ? Twice as much as he had before Job 42:10
Listen I stand ten toes knowing that through Gods grace I am restored
The liquor couldn't save me
Amber
She couldn't save me
Only God could save me and give me back a voice I felt the world stripped from me
It was never my job to jump into the ring
But what happens when you feel no one is there to save you
Listen I could take a few shots and become super woman but that only led to more emotions
Take off the cape
Take off the shades the mask
Take off the gloves
When we realize we don't have to fight , we can rest
Meaning , we no longer need an "escape " to take a break

Postpartum

Postpartum is a lot of things but my biggest one is grief
You grieve your old self before parenthood and I say
parenthood because men go through
postpartum too
Postpartum is grieving the time you no longer have
It's grieving old friendships
It's being angry
Angry because this job was unexpected
Angry because you did not feel prepared
Angry for choosing someone else's life over yours
But knowing you can't live without them
Or being tired to the point where you can't think
Leaving keys in the door
Dishes have piled up
Laundry on the edge of the bed until you muster up the
strength or you just sleep on the pile
Postpartum is 2 minute showers
And in those two minutes you cry your eyes out or
worship God but those 2 minutes are vital
because you've probably gone a day or three without a
shower
So you better enjoy it while you can
Postpartum is hormone imbalance
Having the nutrition sucked out of your body and now
you gotta replace it
Postpartum is losing you
And not the whole you but most of you
And figuring out how to redefine you
Postpartum is being afraid to know yourself
Outside of being the doctor, the teacher, the therapist,

the chef, the driver, the stylist, the
handyman
It's tiring
And it's exhausting
Postpartum is being scared that something could
happen to your kids so you barely sleep
Postpartum is one hell of a thing but if I did not have my
thing one and thing two, I don't even
think I'd be here
So postpartum is also being happy to the point you can't
contain it
Postpartum is learning a strength within you that you
didn't even know existed
Postpartum is finding that new version of you and falling
in love with yourself all over again

Garden

Someone asked me how does my garden grow
By the water
Allowing the waves of life to soak my wounds and
replenish my spirit
Then with therapy once a week
But also filling my week with those who will pluck my
weeds
Want to know what I mean?
People who will tell me there is no such thing as fear
Shania you are strong and you are courageous
Shania stop playing with your own potential
Brothers and sisters who will care for my children
Tending to them during my mental health days
I couldn't grow my garden alone
If I wanted a small garden I could but knowing that God
gifted me a garden to nurture
thousands, I need a village to help me do it
A village who will dig me up out of my blankets when
the depression is setting in and my garden
is wilting
My garden grows far and wide
Into rivers and no matter how much baggage I have
It flows back to me in different currents
Current relationships
Current projects
At least I know my weeds are being pulled by others
and myself so THIS garden will always
continue to grow

I see you

Sweetie , baby
Pick your head up
Fix your crown
Wipe the tears that you cry
Understand that problems have seasons and you'll be
okay
I'm sorry
Can I be the one to apologize to you
I am sorry
To give you the closure that you may never get
From him
From her
From your mom
From whomever may have hurt you and took some of
the last little bit of love you have left
We will get through this
together
Together we will overcome
Together we will rise up
Face the hurt
Become better
Break free
Triumph
I'm sorry
I'm so sorry you've been hurting for this long and have
felt no one saw you
But I see you
I see the warrior amongst the battle
In armor from head to toe
I see the one that hasn't given up

That hasn't run away
I'm with you
I stand beside you
With you
We got this

My Space

Journal Section
Now, it is your turn.
Your voice deserves to be heard.

I have created this journal section specifically for you.
This is your corner, your safe space.

Release it. Let it out. Let go to make room for what God
has for YOU.

Journal Prompt: *Where do I come from?*

Journal Prompt: *How does my garden grow?*

Journal Prompt: *What boundaries do I need to set and with whom to protect my peace?*

Journal Prompt: *Where do I come from?*

Journal Prompt: *If my body could speak, what would it say? Do I need to treat it better? If so, how?*

Journal Prompt: *What wounds or memories am I ready to release?*

Journal Prompt: *What emotion am I having trouble expressing? Why?*

Journal Prompt: *What brings me peace and joy?*

Journal Prompt: *What are some things that I have learned in my healing?*

Journal Prompt: *What are some healthier habits that I can create?*

These words are OUR voices. So many of us have life happening or it has happened. In a big
way too. I am proud of you for continuing this thing called life. I hope we all learn to rest and
reset. I hope we all learn that we are not defined by our past.
You are more than enough.
You are capable.
You are deserving.
You are loved.
You are amazing.
Your life matters.
Your testimony is needed.
I can not wait to see you in the next pages.

Xoxo,
Shania Kerina
Founder of Kerina's Place, http://www.kerinasplace.com